ANTARCTIC
Adventures

ANTARCTIC
Adventures

BARTHA HILL

CF4•K

For my infinitely patient husband, Graham,
who was never too busy to advise, proofread
and encourage.

10 9 8 7 6 5 4 3 2 1
© Copyright 2013 Bartha Hill
ISBN: 978-1-78191-135-8

Published in 2013 by
Christian Focus Publications,
Geanies House, Fearn, Tain,
Ross-shire, IV20 1TW,
Great Britain

Cover design by Daniel van Straaten
Cover illustration by Graham Kennedy
Other illustrations by Graham Kennedy
Printed by Bell and Bain, Glasgow

Contents

An Expensive Old Biscuit

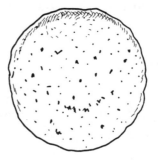

In the year 2011, a 100 year old biscuit sold for £1250 at a British auction. Why would anyone possibly want to pay that much for such an old biscuit? It wasn't even a whole packet, just one biscuit.

It just happened to be one of thousands of such biscuits taken to the Antarctic by an early British explorer, Shackleton, and his companions when they went looking for the South Pole.

In the early 1900s British biscuit makers Huntly and Palmers made many thousands of such biscuits for British Antarctic Expeditions. It was the time when the whole world wanted to know what the bottom of the world beyond the Southern Ocean was really like and many men joined expeditions to go there. The biscuits were specially fortified with milk protein and an important part of the explorers' diets.

For thousands of years, the Antarctic was a mystery to the rest of the world. No one knew whether it was even a single piece of land because the only way to get to it was to cross a fierce, broad ocean current (known as Antarctic Convergence) of the Southern Ocean which surrounds Antarctica.

There were many strange ideas about it: some thought people who went there would have to walk on their heads, or perhaps they just fell off the planet; others thought it was a place where cheerful people lived in a lush green world.

We now know that it is a continent, 99 percent covered in hard ice, and on average 8,000 feet deep. It is about 5.5 million square miles in size, bigger than Mexico and the United States put together, but its actual size and shape change with the seasons. The ice never melts, but sometimes pieces break off and float into the ocean that lies round it. These icebergs are dangerous for ships.

Early explorers like Francis Drake (1570s) and George Shelvocke (1719) got near Antarctica. Shelvocke even said he saw an iceberg, but he never actually found the continent. Then the British Admiralty sent Captain James Cook to look for it. Captain Cook had already explored other parts of the South Pacific Ocean, and he was now commissioned to search a specific area and find out once and for all what was there. His ship was the *Endeavour*, and as well as a crew of ninety-four sailors and a few scientists, he had sheep, pigs, duck, chickens and a goat to provide food for them.

If you have a globe or a map, this is a good time to look at it and trace Captain Cook's journey. Starting from England he sailed round South America to Tahiti. Then he went South to the 40 degree latitude and sailed right along it. He did not see Antarctica but what he did discover was that if it was a continent it was not attached to any of the other continents people knew about. He also mapped the whole coast of New Zealand, Australia and New Guinea.

What he had seen made him want to go back and explore the mystery of Antarctica. So the British Government gave him two ships, the *Adventure* and the *Resolution*, and he set out again, with instructions to start in New Zealand, go as far south as he could and then sail round the 60 degrees south latitude.

Following these instructions, he became the first explorer to cross the Antarctic Circle and see penguins and seals. But he couldn't go as far as he wanted because of icebergs and fierce storms.

He wasn't about to give up. He returned to New Zealand, restocked with food and in December 1773, went back towards the Antarctic. This time, in January 1774, he got to the 70 degrees south latitude, but still didn't see any land.

After this he decided to give up on looking for the continent of Antarctica. His final comments were:

> The risk one runs in exploring a coast in these unknown
> and icy seas is so very great that I can be bold enough
> to say that no man will ever venture further than I have

done, and that the land which lies to the south will never be explored. Thick fogs, snowstorms, intense cold, and every other thing that can render navigation dangerous must be encountered, and these difficulties are greatly heightened by the inexpressibly horrid aspect of the country – a country doomed by nature never once to feel the warmth of the sun's rays, but to lie buried in everlasting snow and ice.

Because of Cook's reports sealers came to the Southern Ocean and killed thousands and thousands of seals. They made a lot of money from their furry pelts.

Even though Cook gave up, many other explorers and seal hunters came and had a look. They saw different parts of the coast of Antarctica, but no one could really say there was a continent rather than individual islands.

Then, in 1831 an explorer called James Clark Ross decided to have a look. James had already explored parts of the Arctic Ocean with his uncle John Ross, and discovered the Magnetic North Pole. He now decided he would like to also find the Magnetic South Pole.

After several trips to the Southern Ocean he reached 78 degrees south latitude and came up against a large ice shelf on the southern side of Antarctica. He studied it for the next two summers. But he didn't land and so didn't succeed in his goal. But he did see a live volcano erupting, spewing fiery red lava onto the sparkling white slopes. He called it Mount Erebus. Mount Erebus is the most southern active volcano in the world but it doesn't erupt very often so he was very fortunate to have seen it.

James Ross went home and for the next fifty or so years people again gave up on Antarctica. Even the sealers didn't come much more as there weren't many seals left.

The biscuit at the beginning of this story could have made the difference between life and death for the person who carried it in his pack. By itself one biscuit isn't worth much, but if it's all the food you have then it could mean life. In 1913, a Commander Evans locked some boxes of these biscuits into a hut before leaving Antarctica. Three years later, a small group of men, desperately hungry, looked in the hut for some food and found none. It turned out many years later that ice had got into the hut and buried the biscuits. The men didn't know that, and hadn't dug deep enough.

Sometimes we feel God is far away and doesn't hear our prayers for help. We forget that God is always there, but sometimes we are not ready to listen, or we don't recognise the answer. We might have to wait.

In the book of Acts, you will find the story of how Peter was thrown in prison. The church prayed 'earnestly' for him. And God gave them an amazing miracle: Peter was released from prison! But as he knocked on the door of the house where they were praying for him, the maid got such a surprise she didn't let him in at first! Pray and trust God to answer when the time is right.

A Remarkable Race

For most of the 19th century the world generally lost interest in Antarctica. Then suddenly at the beginning of the 20th century everyone wanted to claim a piece of Antarctic land.

It began with an international congress held in London in 1895 to make people interested in Antarctica. Because of this, as many as ten countries sent more than twenty expeditions determined to discover what kind of place it really was.

Of course, as these expedition ships tried to push further into the pack ice to reach the shore, some were trapped and several even sank. One ship, called *Belgica*, got caught in the ice and was forced to stay over the winter. They did get out when spring arrived. But not all were that lucky.

By the beginning of the 20th century things began to change. Explorers knew that the weather allowed Antarctic travel only during summer. The best chance to explore the continent was for crews to come in the summer, stay over the winter to prepare and test their equipment, and then set off and explore as soon as summer arrived again.

In 1901, an experienced explorer, Captain Robert Falcon Scott, set out with Ernest Shackleton to look for the South Pole. Their boat was called *Discovery*. They were the first to see a penguin rookery (where penguins nested), set up a base in McMurdo Sound, stayed the winter, and travelled farther south than any explorer had done so far (82 degrees 17 minutes south). They had sledges which they man-hauled instead of using dogs. They tried very hard, but they didn't quite make the Pole. They had learnt a lot, though, and were back in London in 1904.

Five years later, Scott heard that Germany, France, Sweden and Japan were sending expeditions. He certainly wasn't going to let someone else get to the South Pole first! But because he was

worried that others might beat him, he rushed his preparations, cutting back on time for training his men or looking for the very best dogs. He also decided on something new: he took ponies as well as 'motorized' sledges which had never been tested in Antarctic conditions. When he left England in his ship *Terra Nova* on 1st June, 1910 with a crew of sixty-five men, thousands of people cheered him. His last stop before heading for Antarctica was Port Chalmers, Dunedin, New Zealand where he refuelled. Thousands of enthusiastic adults and children came to wave goodbye. The children followed his travels through regular updates in 'The School Journal', a magazine all school children received at school.

What Scott didn't know was that a famous Norwegian explorer called Roald Amundsen had decided to race him for the South Pole on his ship, *Fram*. Amundsen had wanted to be the first person to stand on the North Pole and when someone else beat him to that, he determined to be the first to stand on the South Pole. He prepared very carefully: he read everything he could find about Antarctica. He bought the best dogs from Greenland, fitted them with Arctic designed harnesses and trained them. He chose just nineteen men to come with him and didn't tell them that they were heading for the South Pole. He let them think that they were going to the Arctic. Amundsen didn't tell them that they were going south until they were well on the way and couldn't tell anyone of their destination.

His last refuelling stop was Tasmania and while they were there, he arranged a communication line. Before the *Fram* sailed for Antarctica, Amundsen sent a courtesy message to Scott's base in New Zealand advising him he was heading for

Antarctica but he didn't mention that he was heading for the South Pole!

Exactly ten days after sending that message, Amundsen landed in the Bay of Whales, where he set up his base which he called Framheim. It was about 400 miles from Scott's base. None of the other ships planning to be there actually made it.

For the rest of the summer, both teams made their preparations for the journey to the South Pole. A very important part was to set up a number of depots. A depot was a place to stack food along their planned route. This meant that they didn't need to carry so many supplies, and if they lost the supplies they carried there would be some they could rely on. To make sure that they could find the depots in the snow Amundsen marked his depots with a black flag and dog food, hoping the dogs would find them if his men couldn't. Scott put less food in his depots and spaced them out more than Amundsen.

During the winter both teams prepared their sledges and other equipment, trained their animals, and packed up their food for the journey.

Amundsen's team left their base on 20th October, 1911. Scott headed out on 1st November. He was soon in trouble. The motorized sledges didn't work, and many of the ponies died because the conditions didn't suit them.

Amundsen's team was moving fast. They loved the skiing, which is second nature to Norwegian children. They did have their problems – for example, two members of their team slipped into a crevasse when crossing glaciers and had to be rescued. But soon they were 200 miles closer to the Pole than Scott's men and further south than anyone had ever been.

Scott's team was in much bigger trouble. Fighting violent blizzards and man-hauling the big sledges without the help of ponies, they did manage to get over the Beardmore Glacier.

Although they were both heading for the South Pole, neither team knew where the others were and as they got nearer their goal both kept looking back wondering who was ahead.

At last, on 15th December 1910, Amundsen and his team reached the South Pole. To make sure they had actually reached it they made some careful measurements. For three days they skied to the north, south, west and east, at least ten miles each way and then at angles to make a square. They were absolutely certain that the Pole was somewhere inside that square. They had won the race. They put up the black flag the King of Norway had given them and built a cairn. Then they wrote four notes

to Scott, saluted their flag and set out on the journey back. The pocket knife which Amundsen used to sharpen the bamboo pole to hold the flag, is now in the Canterbury Museum (New Zealand).

On the way back to base they easily found their depots, enjoyed the food and on 26th January, 1911, they were back safely in their hut. After a short rest, they sailed back to Tasmania from where they cabled the king to say they had won the race.

Things weren't so good for Scott and his team. The men were slowed down by illness and weather conditions. Imagine their bitter disappointment when they reached the South Pole and found Amundsen's flag! They had lost the race! Perhaps if they hurried, Scott suggested, they might be the first to get back to base.

Even that turned out to be a disastrous journey. Soon after leaving the Pole they were in terrible trouble. Much of their fuel had vaporised so they couldn't cook, melt water for drinking or warm themselves. They were short of food and suffered from terrible frostbite. Two of his men died. The other three could not get to the next depot because of blizzards and set up a small tent. One of them, Edward Wilson, knew he couldn't go on and didn't want to hold back his mates. So he left the tent, saying, 'I need to go out for a bit, I may be a while.' He never came back, but the other two died soon after anyway.

Amundsen's team took a break in Australia and then went on to New Zealand where he gave lectures about his trip. But until there was news about Scott he could not say for certain he had actually reached the Pole first. It wasn't till the following summer that a search team found Scott and his men and Amundsen could claim his was the first team to reach the South Pole.

When New Zealanders, including the many school children who had followed the adventures of the British team with great enthusiasm, heard the bad news about Scott, they were very sad. Many children wrote letters to Mrs Wilson, the wife of Edward Wilson, who had come to New Zealand to welcome her husband back. Mrs Wilson replied to all of them. Here is her letter to some children from Birkdale School, Auckland, New Zealand. It was later published in the School Journal for all New Zealand children to read:

My dear children

It has been a great help to me to receive your letter of sympathy, and I thank you all. I pray God that the thought of such heroic deaths may help you all to do your best for your country, never mind in how small a way.

The secret of Dr Wilson's heroic end was that all his life he had lived heroically – that is to say, however tired he was, or however busy or however ill he was, he always did everything (little things as well as big things) as perfectly as he could – for in this way he knew he could serve his God and his country; and he prayed every day that he might become more like Jesus Christ our Lord.

His whole life was unselfish; and I know that on this expedition his one thought was to help others in their work. If in any way his life and death can help you boys and girls to be more truthful, kind, and unselfish in your homes, to be more thorough in your work, and to remember that we can never do any big thing in life if we do not do the little things as well as we can; if his death can help you to become more like Jesus Christ, it will help me to bear my great sorrow more than anything else.

I am,

Yours gratefully

Oriana Wilson

To Lose is not Always to Fail

Amundsen had beaten Scott to the South Pole. That was an amazing achievement. It was his goal to do that and every preparation he made was so that he would succeed. It was rather like an athlete who wants to win a gold medal – his whole mind is set on the race and he doesn't allow anything to distract him.

Scott wanted to win that race too, everyone knew that. But he had other things on his mind besides being the first to get to the South Pole. His team had agreed to do a lot of research as well. In this they were successful and many results of their discoveries are still used today.

Here are some of the things his 1910-1912 expedition team did:

Every day the team launched balloons which recorded temperature, wind and barometric pressure data. Scientists still use their records today as a baseline to measure climate changes. These balloons also measured the high-altitude winds that circle the Antarctic continent. It is now known that these winds affect weather around the globe. To get more weather data, Simpson (the team's meteorologist) appointed night watchmen to take readings at midnight as well as noon.

Some of the team took oceanographic measurements which later showed that marine currents, colder than the surrounding water, circle the Antarctic continent. This helped scientists to discover that these currents form a natural barrier that has allowed Antarctic marine life forms to develop along their own paths. Scott's scientists also pulled up dozens of examples of strange, previously unknown, sea life.

Before they left for the Pole, Scott and three others explored the Dry Valleys along the western Antarctic coast. They brought back fish fossils and rocks. They planted flags in the ice and a year later made the first measurements of the movement of the region's glaciers.

Physicist Charles Wright studied how the air and snow together form ice crystals on Antarctic ice sheets. He also studied the nature of icebergs in order to understand how they break off from glaciers and move slowly from the polar ice cap toward the Southern Ocean.

In the midwinter darkness of 1911 three of Scott's men travelled a dangerous 113 kilometres overland each way to retrieve some Emperor penguin eggs. These eggs later helped biologists understand the life cycle of Emperor penguins.

The crew took 40,000 specimens of rocks, corals, freshwater algae, sponges, mollusc, petrels, microbes, worms, lichen, fossilised fish, mummified seal skulls home with them – all collected for the first time and invaluable for research.

Some of this research is only becoming known now, one hundred years later, and scientists are learning to value it.

When Scott set out on this expedition he had no idea that there might be competition and that the whole thing would turn out to be a race. He had received support from many companies who gave him money not only to try and reach the South Pole, but also to do some research. He felt responsible for making sure this was done.

In the first book of the Bible (Genesis) you will find the story of Joseph. Joseph had a hard time, even becoming a slave and was thrown into jail for something he hadn't done. But he never complained. He did the work he was asked to do and he did it the best way he could. When things went wrong for him he didn't ask 'why', rather he thought 'what shall I do now?'

People learnt to trust him and in the end he became the Pharaoh's trusted right hand man, a position of great honour in Egypt.

You may sometimes think that something is 'not fair', that you have done your best, but no one appreciates it. All that matters is that God knows you can be trusted to do the very best you can.

Happy Feet's Story

On the 20th of June, 2011, New Zealander Christine Wilton was walking along her local beach near Wellington with her dog. Suddenly she saw what looked like a bright, shining light among the sand dunes ahead of her. What could that possibly be?

Cautiously she went to investigate. Imagine her surprise when she found herself facing a tall penguin standing on the sand! His sparkling white chest reflected the beams of the late afternoon sun and with his black back he looked as if he was ready for a party.

He flapped his flippers three times and then just stared at Christine. Like most penguins he was not afraid of people as long as they didn't come too close.

He was an Emperor penguin, at 1.1 metres the tallest of all the twenty-two kinds of penguins. The smallest is the Fairy penguin, just 40 centimetres tall. They are all different in looks, size and habits. Although all penguins live south of the Equator, only seven kinds actually live in the Antarctic: Emperors, Chinstraps,

Macaronis, Gentoos, Rockhoppers, Kings and Adélies. They are all great swimmers and catch fish for food.

Christine knew he must have come a long way because Emperor penguins only live in Antarctica and although they swim long distances they only land on ice. To land on a sandy beach in a hot place so far from home meant almost certain death. He was already eating sand and sticks instead of the snow and fish that were his usual diet. Maybe he thought the sand was ice.

He also looked rather hot. The penguin is wonderfully made to fit its environment. Its skin is made up of layers of water-resistant feathers over a layer of woolly down. Under its skin is a layer of fat. All this keeps them safe from the bitter cold. Their black backs and white fronts make them difficult to see by animals who hunt for them: birds from above and whales and other fish from below.

Christine phoned the Department of Conservation immediately. They sent an officer right away. Then she talked to the editor of the local newspaper and it wasn't long before hundreds of people arrived on the beach to see the penguin. The paper invited people to think up a name for him and before long he was known as 'Happy Feet'.

Sadly, Happy Feet began to look very ill and it became quite clear that what he was eating wasn't agreeing with him. He was used to getting ice off a beach, not sand! He would need an operation – at least one, if not more – to clean out his stomach.

He was moved to the Wellington Zoo Hospital where he had several operations to remove stones, sand and sticks from his stomach. Soon he was looking better and was flown to the Christchurch Antarctic Centre Blue Penguin pool to recuperate.

After several days in the freezing temperature and ice he soon began to feel better. But he was too big to stay long among all the little Blue penguins, and as he was quite well again it was decided he should return to Antarctica. But how to arrange that?

Everyone agreed it had to be a place where he would be comfortable. So they looked at how and where Emperor penguins live.

Penguins are birds but they can't fly. To move, they waddle on their feet or slide on their bellies across the snow. This is called 'tobogganing'. They can also jump with both feet together if they want to get somewhere fast. They are wonderful swimmers and spend about half of their lives on land and half in the oceans. Most feed on krill, fish, squid, and other forms of sea-life they catch while swimming under water.

Each penguin family has its own way of breeding. Happy Feet was born in a special rookery which is how all Emperor penguins breed. These 'rookeries' are located on ice, some with millions of birds. The way they breed is remarkable. Happy Feet might have been born in the Auster rookery, set among some spectacular grounded icebergs near Mawson station in Antarctica. About 12,000 Emperor penguins are born there each year.

This is what happens: in early April, when most of the Antarctic's wildlife heads north, and the Antarctic is dark for the winter, Emperor penguins begin their sixty mile (100 kilometre) trek south to their traditional nesting sites on the sea ice. To reach the breeding colony, the birds must cover a huge area of sea ice in pitch darkness (It is winter, remember). Some Emperor colonies contain over 20,000 pairs.

Breeding begins in March, when the new ice is barely thick enough to support their weight. Elaborate courtship rituals take about six weeks and the female lays a single egg on the Antarctic ice in mid-May. She then leaves to spend the winter at sea.

The male is left behind. He scoops the egg onto his feet and under a thick fold of skin, and settles down to wait. For sixty-five days, in temperatures down to -45°C and blizzards up to 200 kilometres per hour, he incubates the egg. He keeps as still as possible and huddles close to his fellow penguins to conserve body heat and turn their backs on the constantly shifting winds. During all this time (about two months) he eats nothing, and only has snow to drink. As a result, he loses 40 percent of his body weight. Not all the males can endure this. Some abandon their eggs and head for the sea to feed.

For those that stick it out, relief comes with the return of the females in mid-July, just as the chick is hatching. With amazing

accuracy, partners recognize each other's calls amongst the thousands of others, and the chick is transferred to the mother's feet and pouch. When the chicks are born, the birds still huddle together as much as possible. While she feeds it regurgitated fish whenever it is hungry, the male is free to go and find his first meal in four months. But it's not easy: he first has to make the two-day journey across 100 kilometres of pack ice to the open sea. When he gets there, he may have to dive to over 300 metres to find food.

After three weeks he returns to relieve the female again. The chicks stand on the adults' feet until they are about eight weeks old, hiding under a brood pouch, or flap of skin, for extra warmth and protection. Older chicks rely on their dense, fluffy feathers and the warm bodies of fellow chicks to keep them warm while their parents look for food.

Soon the chicks are big enough to be left in crèches so that both parents can bring food to them. By mid-December, they have reached 60 percent of their adult body weight, shed their fluffy down for a smart dinner suit and are ready to try their luck in a new environment, the sea. Although about 30 percent of them don't make it this far, those that do have a good chance of living at least 20-30 years.

All that takes about nine months – exactly the same time the annual freezing and break-up of the pack ice takes. Now I'd call that a miracle!

The Emperor penguins are especially suited for their lifestyle. They have small bills to cut down on heat loss. Much of the warm air that would otherwise be lost in breathing is recycled in their nasal cavities. Closely packed, overlapping feathers cover a thick layer of blubber. Their feet are small to cut down on heat loss.

When the Department of Conservation considered all this there really was no other option but to try and return Happy Feet to Antarctica. They fitted him with a tracker device and put in a specially constructed cooled travel box to travel south by ship. Staff from the Antarctic Centre went with him and when they thought they were near enough for him to find his home, they released him into the sea. He hadn't forgotten how to swim and he soon disappeared.

For a couple of days the tracking signal was strong but then it stopped. It has not started again. What had happened to Happy Feet? Probably no one will ever find out.

In the Bible you will find a story about a young man who decided to leave home and do his own thing. He asked his father for his share of the family fortunes. His father was terribly upset but he gave him the money and didn't stop him from going.

Every day he looked for his boy, hoping that he would come home. The boy had a great time at first. Lots of people wanted to be his friend because he treated them to a life of parties and fun. But his money soon ran out and the 'friends' disappeared. He looked for a job but no one wanted him. A farmer finally gave him a job looking after his pigs. He soon discovered that the pigs got better food than he did.

After a while, he decided to go home and say sorry to his dad. Even his father's slaves had a better life than he did with the pigs. So he escaped.

As he got near home he was afraid. Would his father let him come back? What he didn't know was that his father was waiting and looking and as soon as he spotted his boy he ran towards him. He gave him a huge hug, sent him to wash and had a servant prepare new clothes for him to wear. 'Welcome home, my boy,' his father told him, 'I am so glad you are back.'

Many children learn about God when they are little, but like 'Happy Feet' they stray when they are older and get lost in a wicked world. But God is always waiting for them to decide to come back and be part of his family again.

You might like to look up some information about other members of the penguin family and find out how their features match their habits.

What? Two South Poles?

Have you ever stood at midday with a compass in your hand and marked the line between the north and south? If it was a sunny day – did you find your shadow was not exactly along the same line? That is because the compass doesn't point exactly to the north – it points to the North Magnetic Pole. This is about 1,400 miles from the North Pole.

There is also a South Magnetic Pole, approximately at 64 degrees south and 138 degrees east. If you're not sure just where that is, this is another good time to have another look at your globe and work out that location. However, while the North and South Poles are always exactly in the same place, the North and South Magnetic poles are not. Their exact location constantly changes.

It is important for sea captains to know exactly how much variation they have to allow for in calculating the place where they are. Over the years explorers have drawn many magnetic charts, but to get them right it was necessary for them to clearly understand the magnetic properties of the Antarctic region.

In the year 1831, James Clark Ross, a British explorer, and his uncle, John Ross, discovered the Magnetic North Pole. Ten years later, James decided to find the Magnetic South Pole as well. It wasn't going to be easy, he knew that.

For several summer seasons, he went south and explored the Antarctic Wilderness. He got as far as it was possible to sail by ocean: 78 degrees south latitude where he encountered pack ice. He broke through this, entered what became known as the Ross Sea, and sailed along an ice shelf, later named the 'Ross Ice Shelf', after him. But the South Magnetic Pole was located 160 miles inland and he couldn't find a place to land. That was the last of it for him. It wasn't for another sixty-five years that the Magnetic South Pole was in the news again.

You will remember that one of the explorers in the team that didn't manage to reach the South Pole with Scott in 1901, was a young man called Ernest Shackleton. Shackleton had become ill with scurvy, a deadly disease caused by lack of fresh fruit and vegetables (and therefore lack of vitamin C) in the diet. The illness begins with swollen limbs, bleeding gums and increasing weakness.

Shackleton was so ill with scurvy that he couldn't complete the journey. He was bitterly disappointed and was still determined to be the first in some part of the discovery of Antarctica. He hit on the idea of finding the South Magnetic Pole.

So in 1907 he set up his own expedition with two goals: The South Pole and the South Magnetic Pole. As you know, the South Magnetic Pole is not actually a fixed spot, it is more like a circular area, about 30 miles in diameter and on any particular day, or even time of that day, it moves within that circle. To pinpoint it exactly on any one day needs a specially designed magnetic needle.

The journey was tough, but by the end of that summer, his team reached 85 degrees 55 minutes south latitude. No one had ever got that far south. They planted a British flag and took pictures of themselves near it.

But they didn't have much food left and the weather was against them, so at 88 degrees 23 minutes south latitude, and longitude 162 degrees east they decided to give up. They were only 161 miles from the South Pole. Better get home safely and try again another time. Most of the team started on the journey back. Just three decided to go on for another week.

A week later these three reached the Magnetic South Pole at 72 degrees 20 minutes south latitude, and 155 degrees 16 minutes east longitude. It was only ninety-seven miles from the South Pole. They knew they could not go on to the South Pole without risking their lives, so they decided to leave it at that. At least one part of Shackleton's expedition had been a success. He and his team all sailed home to make plans to try for the South Pole again.

In the Bible, there is a story about a young man who decided to stop travelling when he knew he wasn't going to be able to make the distance. John Mark was the young man who ran away when someone spotted him standing around when Jesus was arrested. Some time later he was with his uncle Barnabas and Paul as an assistant on their first missionary journey. But he couldn't stand the pace and after just a short time, before the really tough part of the journey started, he left Paul and Barnabas and returned to Jerusalem. Paul thought he was cowardly and wouldn't take him with him anymore.

But Mark knew what he could do and didn't want to stick his neck out so soon. Barnabas believed that with some help, his nephew Mark would come right and do a great job. Barnabas was good at that – he had helped Paul when he first became a Christian too.

The result of this difference of opinion was that Barnabas and Paul split up. Paul got Silas to come and help him and Barnabas travelled with John Mark. Barnabas was patient with the young man and it paid off. Mark learnt from him and many years later he even became a trusted friend and a great help to Paul. He also wrote the Gospel of Mark in the Bible.

If you find following Jesus difficult you can learn a lot from John Mark. Don't be afraid to ask God to teach you in a way you can understand and ask Him to help you to obey what He wants you to do.

Barnabas was willing to give him another go and encouraged Mark. This changed Mark and with the help of his uncle he became a great friend and helper, even, in the end, to Paul. He learnt from his mistakes and was used by God in a very special way, so much so that we still remember him today.

Everyone's Favourite Food

As astronauts looked down from their space ship they tried to identify some of the things they saw from way out in space. They could see the continents, the oceans, the Arctic and Antarctic, the Great Wall of China and much more – but they also saw a huge red mass like a ribbon right round Antarctica.

What could that be, they wondered? It turned out to be a huge swarm of 10,000 to 30,000 tiny crustaceans known as krill. Krill are a kind of shrimp which grow to about six centimetres in length and two grams in weight. If they escape being eaten by every animal whose basic food they are, they live until they are six years old. Krill are only found in Antarctica.

But it isn't easy for them to live that long. Nearly every creature living in the Antarctic region – whether under or above the water – loves to eat krill. Huge whales, penguins, albatrosses, leopard seals, fur seals, crabeater seals, squid, icefish, they all love krill. And they eat lots of it. One blue whale, for instance, needs 900 kg of krill to feel full! Many of them are specially designed to catch krill. Crabeater seals, for example, have special teeth to sieve krill; baleen whales have huge arched jaws from which baleen plates hang like curtains, these plates filter krill from the seawater.

There probably isn't any other species as abundant as krill. In a year, the Antarctic seal population eat 63-130 million tonnes of it; whales 34-43 million tonnes, birds 15-20 million tonnes, squid 30-100 tonnes and fish 10-20 million tonnes and so on.

Krill (latin name E. Superba) themselves live off phytoplankton – tiny single celled alga. They are fitted with specially designed 'feeding baskets' which they use to filter the algae from the water. They also eat copepods, amphipods and other tiny zoo plankton (zoo means: animal; plankton means float). In the summer they scrape the green lawn of ice-algae from the underside of pack ice. They use their legs for this – they have lots of legs. Even if they can't find any food they can still survive for 200 days. Aren't they wonderfully made?

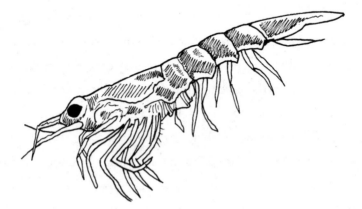

Twice a year female krill lay 2,000-3,000 eggs on the surface of the ocean. These eggs slowly float down about 3000 metres and then hatch. The tiny baby krill slowly float upwards feeding on the yellow part of the egg they were in.

In recent years two things have happened in Antarctica to endanger krill. The first we know as global warming. Krill need pack ice structures to survive. Pack ice forms natural cave-like features which krill use to escape predators. With less pack ice, the numbers of krill go down dramatically. When there are fewer krill many of the animals who depend on them for food will go hungry and die.

The second problem is in two parts and has to do with fishermen. Krill makes great fish bait as well as nourishing food for other animals. South Korea, Norway, Japan, Russia and Poland come to the Antarctic specially to catch krill for this purpose.

As if this wasn't enough to endanger the krill population, scientists discovered that krill are very high in Omega 3 fatty acids which many people use as medication. At first it wasn't possible to catch krill and take it away from Antarctica because it didn't keep. But modern ships are being developed to catch krill and process them immediately. As you can imagine, this has a terrible effect on the krill population. And because of this it also affects animals who live on krill – for example, penguins.

The story about krill reminds us of Adam and Eve in the Garden of Eden. God had given them a beautiful place to live, with work to do and plenty of delicious and nourishing food to eat. But there was one tree they were not allowed to touch. They certainly weren't permitted to eat the fruit of the tree of the knowledge of good and evil (Gen. 2:17).

But when the serpent came along and asked Eve why she wasn't eating the fruit of that tree, suddenly Eve couldn't think of anything better to eat. All of a sudden she wondered if she had perhaps got it wrong: God would never have stopped them from eating something so luscious and beautiful? A little bit wouldn't hurt, she thought. So she took one of the fruit off the tree and bit into it. It tasted so good that she ran to find Adam. This is a wonderful fruit, she told him, here, try it. And Adam did.

God wasn't happy about what they had done. They knew he wouldn't be, so when it was time for their daily garden walk with God, they hid under the scrub. God soon found them.

He told them they had disobeyed him and so they could no longer live in his garden. He threw them out of his garden. Now they had to drill for water, sow seeds and weed the plants, and hunt if they wanted meat. There was no going back. Life became hard.

But God loved them and he loves you. God has given humanity a message of hope, the gospel – a message that promises that all those who believe in the Lord Jesus Christ will be saved. One day God will give his people 'the right to eat from the tree of life, which is in the paradise of God' (Rev. 2:7) and we will 'have the right to the tree of life and may go through the gates into the city' (Rev. 22:14).

Everything he made will then be back in balance and his children will be allowed to enjoy them.

The Story of Mrs Chippy

On the first of August 1914, a ship by the name of *Endurance* got ready to sail from the docks in London for Antarctica. On board, with a special mission, were Ernest Shackleton and his team.

Once the South Pole had been reached, British explorer Ernest Shackleton came up with a new idea: he would be first to cross Antarctica from one coast of the continent to the other on foot with dogsleds. That was a journey of 1800 miles (3000 km) over land from the Weddell Sea to the Ross Sea.

Shackleton raised funds for two ships: *Aurora* and *Endurance*. Shackleton himself sailed in *Endurance*, planning to establish a base somewhere around the Weddell Sea and start out from there. *Aurora*, under Captain Mackintosh, was to sail to the Ross Sea, find a base in or near McMurdo Sound, and from there lay supply depots for the second half of Shackleton's journey. The *Aurora* left Sydney, Australia on the 24th of December 1914.

Shackleton advertised in Britain for helpers and was astonished that five thousand men wanted to come with him. It was quite a challenge to choose only twenty-seven! He also chose sixty-nine dogs whom he thought would be the key to a successful expedition. The *Endurance* sailed in August 1914, headed for the Weddell Sea.

On board *Endurance* was a crew member Shackleton knew nothing about. When the ship's carpenter Henry McNeish opened his toolboxes, he got a big surprise! A large cat lay curled up in one of his boxes. McNeish decided that a cat as determined to travel as that should be allowed to come. But he didn't say anything about it until they were well out to sea.

Actually when he heard about it, Shackleton was quite pleased to have a cat on board to keep mice and rats under control. The cat became known as Mrs Chippy (carpenters were often called

'chippies') and it wasn't till much later that someone discovered Mrs Chippy was actually a tom cat. By then it was too late to change his name. All the sailors loved him, but no one more than the carpenter who had brought him on board.

Mrs Chippy did a good job catching rats and mice before they could get at the provisions. The caged dogs weren't happy about him. Every day he tormented them by sitting on top of their kennels, mewing loudly and sharpening his claws on the roofs. Then he moved to a place where they could see him and calmly washed himself. Then he watched while the dogs barked loudly.

But mostly he just got on with his job and the sailors loved him for that.

The *Aurora* team had landed at Cape Evans in January 1915. Summer in Antarctica that year was unbelievably awful making the work of the depot laying teams almost impossible. But they

were determined and in spite of hunger, frostbite, scurvy and total exhaustion they managed to lay the four depots Shackleton had asked them to do. In May, everyone moved on board to get through the winter. Unfortunately, a ferocious blizzard blew the ship away with most of their provisions, leaving some of the team on shore. There was no way to reach them again. The abandoned men did find some food and equipment left behind by other expeditions, so they survived two winters hoping that someone would come to rescue them one day. The *Aurora* limped back to New Zealand for repairs.

In the mean time, Shackleton's camp on the other side of the continent was also suffering. Winds with speeds of 100 miles per hour threw them about, the temperature was as low as -57° C and huge icebergs larger than football fields floated around them. The *Endurance* was trapped in the ice of the Weddell Sea and stayed that way all winter. Shackleton did his best to keep his team happy with sports, board games, music and dog races. His scientists observed the stars and recorded valuable information about wildlife and weather. Mrs Chippy did not like ice. It got stuck between his toes and pads and so he confined himself to the ship.

After 326 days, the boat finally came free of the ice, but now there was another problem. The ice twisted around the boat and looked as though it might crush it. Shackleton ordered his men to get the supplies and lifeboats off the ship and put them on a huge ice floe beside it. They pitched tents and called it 'Ocean Camp'. Mrs Chippy sat on a box and watched nervously. They had barely finished when the ice moved in even further and completely crushed the ship's hull, totally wrecking the ship. It finally sank at the end of November.

Shackleton knew that with the loss of the ship his hope of crossing the Continent was now gone and he turned his mind to working out how to save the lives of his men. The three lifeboats they had were their only hope. He ordered the men to load their supplies on board the small boats. Last up was Mrs Chippy. He wasn't about to be left behind!

For seven days they searched for ways out of the ice, and after many death defying adventures the three crews landed on a rocky beach called Elephant Island. It was now 15th April, 1916. It was a lonely place and only penguins and seals lived there. Shackleton knew that no one would ever think to look for his team on such a remote island. Somehow he had to find a way to civilization.

He knew that Elephant Island was 800 miles from a whaling station called South Georgia. The whalers would have the ships and experience to help them. But such a journey was perilous: it was already winter, they would travel on the open ocean, their sextant wouldn't work well on overcast days – it would be easy to miss the small island altogether. But what other hope was there? The carpenters on the crew had already used one of the lifeboats to make a hut, but the other one, the sturdy James Caird, might be their only chance.

With a heavy heart, Shackleton chose five crew members to come with him and promised the others he would come back for them. Sadly, there wasn't room for Mrs Chippy.

Sailing the small boat was exhausting and fraught with danger. It was freezing cold, and they had hardly any food. But after an epic fifteen days at sea they spotted South Georgia on the horizon! They made towards it and landed. Disaster struck when a sudden hurricane wind destroyed their boat not long after they had climbed out of it.

Unfortunately they had landed on the wrong side of the island and there was a 3,000 foot (1,000 metre) mountain between them and the sealers' camp. The only way to get there was to climb over it – a feat of stamina and strength that still defies experts who have tried to climb it. But Shackleton set out with two of his team. After thirty miles of glacier crevasses, snowfields and icy gales they reached the summit and well into the descent they finally heard someone whistle. They knew they must be near the whaling station.

The captain of the Norwegian whaling station, who had heard that Shackleton and his men had all died, was overcome with joy to welcome them when they knocked on the door of his hut.

The whaling station staff immediately got a team together and equipped three boats to go and look for the men Shackleton had left behind. When the men on Elephant Island saw the boats in the distance they rushed to the shore to wave them in. Shackleton counted them – 'They're all there,' he shouted.

Sadly Mrs Chippy had disappeared – possibly he had died trying to escape the terrible cold. Henry McNeish never forgot his friend. He went to work in Welllington, New Zealand, as a carpenter and many years later when he died, some people had a special bronze statue made of Mrs Chippy and placed it on his grave. He will never be forgotten!

Shackleton didn't forget the Ross Sea team. The rescuers sailed south and you can imagine the joy of the *Aurora* team when they saw them coming!

It was going to be many years before someone tried again to cross Antarctica.

Shackleton had a dream – he wanted to be the first to cross Antarctica on foot, but never got to do it. But he promised his men that he would come back and rescue them, and he did.

If we give our lives to Jesus we have his promise – one day we will be together with him in heaven. Whatever life has to throw at us, whether it be good and meaningful times or hard and painful times we are 'kept by Jesus'. He will always be waiting for us to come back when we fall.

And he will keep his promise.

Rations, Remedies and Rubbish

Spending time in Antarctica is so different to spending time anywhere else in the world. People who go there have to be prepared to melt ice to get drinking water, bring their food and medicines and special clothes to keep the icy cold out. So it is not surprising that explorers invented many things to make it easier.

COOKING

To melt ice, cook food and give light in the pitch dark winter months was a number one priority and led to the discovery of the 'Primus' stove, from the Greek word for 'first'. Until recently, everyone who went camping had one of these, but it took quite a while to develop.

Early travellers to the Arctic used small oil lamps with wicks to cook food. With the low heat output it took a lot of their time to cook meals: time which they would rather spend on exploring the continent. In 1881 a member of a United States

Polar Expedition, Lieutenant A W Greely, introduced a primitive stove that fitted over a burner. It was certainly better than the lamps they had used until then.

Then a man called Fridtjof Nansen, who was planning to cross the Greenland Ice Cap for the first time, thought he could do better. He developed a portable stove that could not only cook but at the same time melt snow.

Nansen's cooker was made of copper and was covered in thick felt. It stood over a lamp and drew the heat up through a narrow pipe around which a much wider space formed the food area. On top of the pipe a container with snow in it melted. It turned out to work well for the snow, but did not produce hot water.

A Stockholm toolmaker took on the challenge of developing a more efficient cooker and the result was a stove that ejected fuel under pressure. This resulted in a much hotter flame. It was made of aluminium and stainless steel he called 'Primus'. Nansen put it to the test in his 1893 expedition and found that food cooked faster and not only that, it used less fuel. It now became standard equipment for polar expeditions. It certainly helped to make the explorations of the Antarctic possible.

REMEDIES

A well equipped medical kit was something every early Antarctic explorer needed. In 1910 Burroughs Wellcome and Co, London, a leading supplier of medicines, designed a medical box for the British Antarctic Expedition. It measured just 169 mm by 140 mm by 140 mm. For such a small box it contained a surprising number of medicines and lotions. It was all the early explorers

carried, because there were no doctors or other medical help available, there was no radio base to call for help, nor any kind of hospital to go to. Nowadays sick people working in Antarctica can be flown out if necessary; that wasn't possible in those days.

So only the medical kit often stood between life and death.

What was in the medical kit? Probably not what would be in such a box today, but it was put together by the best doctors of the time. They were all carefully labelled to make sure explorers knew what to use when they had a problem.

There was boric acid and tannin for burns (often acquired during cooking), digitalis tincture for heart problems, gelsemium tincture for coughs, sodium bicarbonate, chalk powder, calcium lactate and soda mint for upset stomachs, sodium salicylate for general aches and pains, soothing lotions: hazeline cream, opium tablets for pain or diarrhoea, vegetable laxative for constipation, zinc sulphate and cocaine for eye wash, and many other medicines and lotions.

There were needles, pins, bandages, gauze and dressings as well as some instruments – a beard clipper and a pair of dental forceps (not hard to imagine what those might be for!), scalpels to drain wounds, various probes and tweezers to help manage wounds that often occurred while working with the sledges, heavy equipment and stoves.

And all that in one small box!

RUBBISH

In early times explorers often left their marks on the unspoiled landscape of Antarctica by not taking their rubbish with them when they went home. This all changed in 1985-1986 when Captain Robert Swan suggested that people who came to Antarctica should leave only their footprints behind, everything else should be packed in bags and brought back to where it had come from. So each of their sleds not only carried their food and equipment, it also had a special place for any rubbish left from each meal and camp. There should be nothing left to show they had been there. And that is generally the rule for everyone who visits Antarctica or lives there for a time.

In the book of Genesis (Gen. 1:28) we read that when God had created man He made him to 'rule over' everything He had made. That means that He expected Adam and Eve to take responsibility for the environment and the other creatures that share our planet. We must not be wasteful as we do this. God gave us a wonderful world and we must not be careless in the way we look after it. A great many parts of the world have been spoiled, so it is doubly important that we take care of this beautiful unspoiled part of the world.

Byrd Eyes the South Pole

About the same time Scott first tried to get to the South Pole (1901-1904) and didn't make it, aircraft were being discovered. In 1914, two years after Amundsen beat Scott in a race to the Pole, airplanes were being used in the First World War.

Once the war was over (1918) pilots needed new challenges. Already Americans were designing planes that could fly longer distances. On the 9th of May, 1926, pilots Richard Byrd and Floyd Bennett claimed to be the first to have flown over the North Pole. But flying across the South Pole, now that was another story!

Richard Byrd dreamt of being the first man to fly over the South Pole. He knew that one pilot had already tried it: in 1928 Hubert Wilkins had flown over 1,000 kilometres of Antarctica in order to take pictures.

Richard realised that to fly all the way across Antarctica would be much more difficult and need a lot of preparation. He would have to find ships to take the planes there and men to build runways. They had to learn how to look after the aircraft and practise flying in the very dangerous conditions. But he loved a challenge!

It took him three years to put together the largest and most ambitious expedition to Antarctica so far. He bought two ships and three aircraft. He had the aircraft stripped down, lightened and specially adapted for cold weather high altitude flying. Clothes and food for this massive expedition included 1,200 pairs of boots, 2,000 pairs of socks, 500 crates of eggs, 1,200 lbs (544.32 kgs) of cookies and much, much more!

Byrd and his men arrived in Dunedin, New Zealand at the beginning of the southern summer of 1928. They stocked up

on last minute stores before setting off in terrible weather for Antarctica. The voyage down to the Southern Ocean was long and difficult but the ships carrying the planes finally got through the pack ice on Christmas Day.

Byrd had to be very careful about the place to set up his winter quarters, for not only did he have a large team to accommodate, there were three aeroplanes to be housed, as well as food, tools, instruments and fuel. He also needed a level and stable area of ice to build a landing strip for the planes. It was Antarctica's first village and when it was finished he called it Little America.

Progress was steady and on the 15th of January 1929, they were ready for the first trial flight. The engine and engine oil were

heated by a torch and the icicles cleared from the ailerons. With eight men hanging on to the wings when it taxied cross-wind, the Fairchild monoplane taxied down the hard ice runway and took off. A few minutes later the crew could hardly believe their eyes. During the hour they were in the air, they had the most wonderful panoramic views of 1,000 square miles (2,590 kilometres) of Antarctica anyone (except Wilkins) had ever seen. They took many photographs and made careful notes of what they saw.

But it wasn't easy. Their compasses didn't work because they were so close to the Magnetic Pole and the glare from the ice was blinding. Because it was near impossible to judge distances, landing was very difficult. But they made it.

It was nearly two weeks before they made another flight. This time they spotted a range of mountains no one had ever seen before. They flew along the fourteen peaks and called them the Rockefeller mountains. How much more could be discovered from a plane, they thought.

Before winter, three of the geologists on the team flew to these mountains to collect some rock samples. They successfully landed and did their work. Then, as they were about to take off, a storm arrived. They sent a message to the base to say that they would take off as soon as the weather cleared. But day after day there was no change. Everyone in Little America was worried when no more messages came.

Nine days later there was a break in the weather. A search party set off in another plane. It was dangerous and frightening, but it was the only chance they had of finding the missing men. As they flew and searched, they finally saw what looked like a roughly made landing with flags. The plane bounced, lurched and almost cartwheeled as the pilot worked to land it. As soon as they landed, three men came running over the ice and snow to greet them.

It was too late to fly back so they all squashed into the tent and heard the story. Although the geologists had tied the plane down with strong ropes, a wild gust tore them loose, leaving the plane hanging on only by its ice anchors. When another strong gale freed it the plane flew backwards for half a mile and then crashed against the side of a mountain. It was obvious it would never fly again.

Fortunately the weather soon cleared enough for the rescuers and the geologists to fly back to Little America.

Winter set in soon after that and there was no more flying until Spring came. In the total darkness, the men worked to prepare for the flight they had come to Antarctica for. Because of the dangers of flying there would be two ground parties who could rescue them if they crashed. The plane would make two trips: the first to leave supplies halfway and look for a good route, the second flight would go all the way to the Pole.

The ground parties left in mid October and a month later, the plane took off. The weather was glorious and all went well; they found an excellent place to land and they quickly unloaded cans of gasoline and oil as well as bags of food. Soon they were back in the sky.

Another drama! The fuel tanks were less than a quarter full! It turned out that on the way out the radio operator had found a leak at the bottom of the hand operated fuel pump and plugged it with chewing gum. It had worked well at first, but now it clearly was not. They needed to get back to base fast.

About a hundred miles from base the engines cut out and the plane spiralled down, miraculously landing gently on a piece of level land. Their radio call for help soon brought their second plane with fuel to get them back to base.

It was not till the 28th of November that the plane was fixed and the weather was good again for flying. They had a heavier load this time – some heavy aerial camera equipment plus fuel and food had been packed away in the hold.

They did well at first but then had to cross the high mountains. The plane was too heavy to get over them so they had to make a difficult decision: if they jettisoned fuel they wouldn't have enough left to get them to the Pole and back, if they jettisoned food they would almost certainly die from starvation if they had to make a forced landing. After a long discussion everyone agreed that some food would have to go. At least they then had a chance of getting back to base.

As soon as the load lightened the plane rose and just cleared the mountains. The Pole was just ahead of them. They circled over it, taking careful measurements and photos.

They were back in Little America early in the morning of 29th November, sixteen hours after they had left. In the space of one day they had achieved what had taken Amundsen three months on foot.

During the rest of the summer they concentrated on taking aerial photographs. Then they headed home. Were there to be any more firsts for Antarctica?

In this story you learnt how Admiral Byrd had a goal he wanted to achieve. He wanted it so badly that he put his whole mind on getting it. Olympic gold medallists don't just go out and run or jump – they spend many hours, days and years practising their sport and getting fit to reach their goal.

You don't have to be a great pilot or an athlete, but God expects that you run the race he has set up for you and reach the goals he has planned for us. They are specially designed for each of his children, and he has given them the gifts they need to achieve them. In the book of Hebrews, chapter 12, we read:

Therefore, since we are surrounded by such a great cloud of witnesses, let us throw off everything that hinders and the sin that so easily entangles, and let us run with perseverance the race marked out for us. Let us fix our eyes on Jesus, the author and perfecter of our faith, who for the joy set before him endured the cross, scorning its shame, and sat down at the right hand of the throne of God (Heb. 12:1-2).

Magnetic Games

The sky over Antarctica is dark for four months of every year. Morning, afternoon, evening and night are all the same – dark. But every now and then, magnetic forces play with winds from the sun and light up the sky with a fantastic game of colours. This is called Aurora Australis – meaning 'southern lights'. It also happens at the North Pole, where it is called Aurora Borealis ('northern lights'). Many Antarctic explorers saw this exquisite dance of multicoloured lights plunging, sweeping, swirling and shimmering across the dark sky.

It's all to do with the Magnetic Poles. You know that there is a strong magnetic field around earth and that this can confuse a ship's captain's compass. Whenever the sun experiences magnetic storms it sends out a solar wind of light particles which blow towards the earth. These particles collide with gases in the earth's atmosphere and make them glow with red, green, blue and violet lights. They are strongest and most spectacular in the Polar regions.

A member of the 1901 expedition saw Aurora Australis and wrote a description for the New Zealand School Journal in May 1912. He told how the Antarctic winter night, four months long, was 'a severe ordeal' and made more trying because of the terrible blizzards.

Then he says:

… About seven o'clock one evening in June, 1903, I was quietly skiing along over the frozen sea about a mile and a half south of the *Discovery*. The night was intensely dark. I was moving slowly northwards when my attention was abruptly arrested by a bright blue patch of light that suddenly appeared in the sky behind the mighty dome of Mount Erebus, whose outline now showed as plainly as in daylight. A moment and the light was gone. I stopped and looked with wondering eyes on the strange sight. Then in several points of the north and north eastern sky pale patches of swiftly moving green light rapidly showed for a few moments and then disappeared. Almost at once two arcs of light appeared, one above the other, with a faint yellowish tinge and with their lower edges sharply defined against the dark sky. From their upper edges rays of light leaped upwards – now approaching the zenith, now retreating wildly; now closing into one body, then opening out again. The lower edge of the lower arc was now tinted with prismatic colours. A swift play of light went on for some minutes; then as suddenly as the light had come it disappeared. At intervals this weird performance continued for an hour. It was a display of the Aurora Australis that I had witnessed.

If you live in the northern part of the northern hemisphere or in the southern part of the southern hemisphere you can check the internet (www.spaceweather.com) to find out when there is a magnetic storm on the sun and keep an eye out for an Aurora a day or two later.

Have you ever read the first verses in the Bible? In Genesis 1:1-3 we read:

> In the beginning God created the heavens and the earth. Now the earth was formless and empty, darkness was over the surface of the deep, and the Spirit of God was hovering over the waters. And God said, 'Let there be light,' and there was light. God saw that the light was good, and he separated the light from the darkness. God called the light 'day' and the darkness he called 'night'. And there was evening, and there was morning, the first day.

That gives you a feeling for what it is like in the Antarctic winter – all dark – before God made the light of day. You couldn't live in one hundred percent darkness, so before he made man, God made light. Thank him for the light today.

The Secret Land

In January 1947, the *USS Currituck*, an American ship, was lying at anchor off the Shackleton Ice Shelf on the Queen Mary Coast of Wilkes Land. On board were three American aircraft on photographic missions.

One day, Lieutenant Commander David E. Bunger, plane commander of one of the planes, took off as usual. As he flew south and towards the coast, his flight crew noticed a dark spot on the pure white horizon. They headed towards it and couldn't believe their eyes – there before them was a land of blue and green lakes and brown hills surrounded by ice.

Wondering if they were dreaming, they made careful notes so they would remember exactly where they were and what they saw. They also took photos of the amazing scene they saw below them. Then they went home to tell others what they had seen.

A few days later, the weather was again suitable for flying so Bunger and his flight crew went back, this time in a 'flying boat', for another look. It was real, they hadn't dreamt it. One of the lakes looked big enough for them to land on. Bunger carefully landed his plane on it and slowly came to a stop.

The lake was filled with blue, green and red algae which gave the lakes their colour. Was this perhaps the result of global warming, the men wondered. They rolled up their sleeves and dipped their arms in the lake. They didn't have a thermometer to measure how warm it was, but they did have a bottle. They filled this with water from the lake. It proved to be rather warmer than the icy waters in other parts of the Antarctic, and salty, a sign that it wasn't an inland lake but an arm of the open sea.

It wasn't the only lake either: there were several others, some with fresh water, others with salt water. The largest and deepest lake, Algae Lake, was 25 kilometres long and about 137 metres deep. It was a spectacular place, surrounded by glaciers but free of ice throughout the year, and they called it Bunger's Oasis.

There are some times when Jesus surprises us with his love. Can you think of a time when you were surprised because of something special that happened to you? Did you think it might be a special present from Jesus to you?

The Bible says that Paul prayed that the people of Ephesus would 'grasp how wide and long and high and deep is the love of Christ, and to know this love that surpasses knowledge ...'

When something special happens to you, think how much Jesus loves you and remember to thank God for his gifts to you.

Another First

More than forty years after Shackleton gave up on crossing the Antarctic continent on foot, someone else decided to have a go.

In 1948, British explorer Vivian Fuchs made a survey trip to the Falkland Island Dependencies. He camped on Alexandra Island and made that his base. But the weather was dreadful and at times severe blizzards forced him to stay in his tent.

While waiting for the weather to improve so he could get on with his job, he found himself thinking about Antarctica and crossing the continent on foot. Could he possibly do that when no one else had managed it? To amuse himself while waiting for the weather to improve he worked out what he might need.

Two teams, just like Shackleton had would be essential, he thought. One of these teams would start from the Weddell Sea and head for McMurdo Sound in the Ross Sea, crossing the Continent via the South Pole, a journey of nearly 3,000 kilometres. Fuchs himself would of course lead that team.

The other team would start in McMurdo Sound, and lay food and fuel depots along the second part of Fuchs' journey between the Pole and McMurdo Sound. They would then go back to their base. Both teams would use mechanical Sno-cats and Ferguson farm tractors as well as dogs. He would have to start by finding a second leader. After a lot of thought he decided that New Zealand explorer Edmund Hillary, the first man to climb Mount Everest, might be his man. It all began to feel real. He decided to get hold of Hillary as soon as he got off Alexandra Island and back to London.

It so happened that Hillary was in London when Fuchs arrived there in 1953 and the two men met up. Fuchs told him about the plans he had worked out. 'There will be three stages to the adventure,' he said. 'The first stage will be a trip to the Weddell Sea (1955) to get a feel for the land and what we will be up against. The second stage is for both of us and the rest of the team to then return home to raise support. We will return to Antarctica for the attempt to cross Antarctica in the summer of 1957 – that is the third stage. In the mean time, a wintering party of eight will stay behind in Antarctica and have things ready for us when we get back.'

Hillary loved adventure and this journey sounded very exciting to him. He signed up and in London on the 14th of November, 1955, he boarded the steel hulled expedition ship, *Theron*, specially built for work in ice.

They arrived at the Weddell Sea a few days before Christmas. Fuchs had hoped to find a new route to the main land from there. But it didn't all go as smoothly as they had planned. Almost immediately their ship froze in the ice. The crew hacked away at the ice with picks, shovels and even explosive charges, but they couldn't find a way through.

By the middle of January it became clear that their only hope was to give up the search for a new route. The end of the Antarctic summer was coming close and they absolutely had to unload the equipment for the crew who were staying behind for the winter. So they found a tongue of ice that looked strong enough to support all the gear. As fast as possible they began to unload what they would need to set up a base there.

That wasn't the end of their troubles, though. With high seas pounding the ship all of a sudden, a huge mass of floating ice crashed into the ship's side. It tore off the anchors and the ship whirled away out of sight. Now everyone was stranded on the ice.

Fortunately, after a while the storm eventually blew the ship back. Fuchs ordered everyone to board before it got away again. The ship then moved to the centre of the bay to ride out the storm.

Twenty four hours later Fuchs decided to try once more to offload the cargo. The men climbed down from the ship and worked frantically – this might be their last chance. On the 7th of February the job was finished.

Later that day the captain spotted another lot of pack ice heading in their direction, so before the ship could be locked in again, Fuchs gave the order to sail.

The eight men to be left behind looked lonely and forlorn as they waved the ship goodbye. There wasn't a lot of time to feel sorry for themselves though: they had to build themselves winter quarters and shelter for the 300 tonnes of gear.

While they were thinking about building their quarters they used the crate their Sno-cat had come in as a shelter for the time being. It worked out so well, they decided not to build another place to live in. There wasn't time anyway: the blizzards were so intense that they could hardly move all the stores and the tractors kept breaking down. A particularly violent blizzard swept away 300 drums of fuel, all their coal, most of their building timber and a Ferguson tractor. It was going to be a very long and difficult winter.

But somehow they managed to do everything they had been asked to do. When the main expedition returned in November 1956 the radio connection was installed, the dogs were trained and the men had even found a route for Fuchs and the team to start off their trip to the Pole.

In 2 Corinthians 11 you will read how Paul told his readers about some of the terrible things he had gone through during his four missionary journeys. He was in prison and flogged, beaten with rods; he was shipwrecked, often hungry and thirsty, and suffered many other terrible things. Yet in chapter 12, he tells how he learnt that when he was at his neediest, Jesus came to him and gave him strength. It didn't mean bad things didn't happen; but when they did, Jesus was there for him.

Are you starting a new school, moving to a new country, playing a difficult match – whatever your challenge – he is always there for you too; ask him to help you.

Every Bit Counts

While the team of eight were working through the winter in Antarctica, both Fuchs and Hillary were at home trying to raise enough money for the main expedition.

Fuchs raised money the way British expedition leaders had always done: he asked for help from research groups and companies interested in Antarctica and from the Government.

Hillary had to start from scratch. He knew that New Zealanders had always been interested in Polar exploration. They had often helped expeditions with goods and services when they called in at the New Zealand southern ports of Christchurch and Dunedin as a last stop before heading for the Pole.

But to find money for this huge project? It was a big challenge for a small country.

He began by asking the Government for their support. New Zealand owned Scott Base in Antarctica and gave him permission to use that as his base. The Government also gave $50,000. Hillary had to find the rest ($100,000) in some other way.

Hillary knew that in England big companies sponsored expeditions, but he didn't think that would work in New Zealand.

He also really wanted to involve everyone in his project. So he got a team of seven hard working people together to develop a strategy.

This team immediately began work. After all, there wasn't much time! They set up sixty-seven centres in New Zealand. Each centre was given a target according to their size and invited to set up a local committee to raise the money allocated as its share in the venture. The Mayor of every city and borough in New Zealand wrote support letters to the committee in their area.

The appeal was officially launched by the Prime Minister on 10th October, 1955. It captured the imagination of New Zealanders who loved the idea of one of their own people, especially national hero Ed Hillary, leading an exciting expedition to Antarctica.

In each area groups began to look for ways to raise money, and it wasn't just adults who wanted to help. Schools and community groups wanted to be in on the project and children got behind it with their own ideas. It became a competition!

Soon money began to come in. New Zealand children all knew about Hillary's conquest of Mount Everest and it wasn't long before schools got behind this new venture. Some sponsored huskies, giving them a name of their choice, for £50 each. Wellington Boys' College raised money for a dog as well as a sled (£150). Young women earned money by babysitting and sent it in. Community groups ran dances, film evenings and street stalls.

Children paid to come to lectures Hillary and other speakers gave, and did school projects about Antarctica. Three Masterton children reared guinea pigs and sold them. Two boys from Lower Hutt sold tadpoles for tuppence each and made £2.10 for the fund.

A man called George Emmus suggested they get some rock from McMurdo Sound, have it cut up and sell the pieces as paper weights. They were able to get 1.5 tons (1.4 tonnes) of rock from near Scott's hut and have it brought back to New Zealand. The paper weights were an instant success: everyone wanted one!

There were trade tables, Antarctic displays, silver trails, film evenings, street days, parties, auctions of gifted items, and more. All of these raised money. Everyone worked hard to reach the target set for their region and nearly everyone reached their goal in good time.

But the people of New Zealand didn't just give money. Many firms and industries helped with equipment or supplies of all kinds. Oil and petrol, clothes and food, blankets, photographic equipment, toothpaste and soap, slippers and gumboots all came in as donations.

A very special gift offer came from tractor maker Massey-Ferguson Ltd, who made five Ferguson tractors available. They were standard, although small, farm tractors adapted by their engineers for Antarctic conditions.

While all this was happening, Hillary selected a site on Mount Cook, New Zealand's highest mountain, to train the dogs he intended to take with him. He knew that one of the problems with dogs in the past had been that they weren't properly trained for the job they were asked to do. With New Zealand not too far from Antarctica he could train dogs in the mountain snows and get them to their destination without them losing too much of their conditioning.

Everything was ready by December and on 1st January, 1957 Hillary and his team arrived in McMurdo Sound with eighteen men, sixty well trained dogs, seven tractors and a Beaver reconnaissance plane. A few days later the team's pilot, Bill Cranfield, took Hillary on a flight to have a look at the route they planned to take to the South Pole.

Because Hillary had been in Antarctica at the beginning of that year, he knew what they had to do first. The team set up their winter quarters, took the dogs on training runs, and put in the first two depots. At the end of February their ship returned to New Zealand and the winter season began.

Although Hillary's job was to lay depots for Fuchs' team, he also had a secret ambition for himself. He thought that as long as he did the best possible job for Fuchs, he might just have time to become the first man to drive a tractor all the way to the South Pole.

They worked hard all winter, getting every part of their equipment ready for the big journey and on the 14th of October, Hillary and his team started out for the Pole at almost exactly the same moment, Fuchs and his team set out from the Weddell Sea.

From their nearby base, the Americans waved them goodbye, all the while making fun of the tractors – they thought that compared to their own large tractors the small Fergusons looked fragile and ill equipped to tackle Antarctic conditions. But it turned out that although seemingly small, they were robust and reliable; they happily ploughed through the snow and up steep gradients at temperatures they had never experienced before.

It took Hillary's team two months to set up the depots at the 78th, 80th and 82nd parallels as agreed with the plane, tractors and dogs bringing up fuel and food. It was never easy. There were white-outs, forced landings and times when the plane couldn't take off. Sometimes the tractors slipped into crevasses and were saved by towlines. But one after another the supply dumps were set up until all of them were done.

Hillary knew that Fuchs and his team were not moving as fast as they had planned: there might just be time for him to get to the Pole. His team agreed enthusiastically. Along the way they built cairns every few hundred yards and planted snow flags to mark the snow bridges they found. At last, on the 4th of January, 1958, Hillary and his men arrived at the American laboratory at the Pole.

He turned off his motor and climbed down. The Americans took them into their warm Polar station and fed them with fresh food.

'I took a last look at our Fergusons,' Hillary wrote later. 'They looked lonely and neglected, like broken toys cast aside after playtime. There was no doubt about it, our tractor train was a bit of a laugh! Yet the Fergusons had brought us across twelve hundred and fifty miles of snow and ice, crevasses and sastrugi (long wavelike ridges of snow), soft snow and blizzard. We were the first to drive all the way to the South Pole in tractors.'

Fuchs was still more than 300 miles (483 kilometres) from the Pole. Hillary wondered if he would make it before getting caught by winter. But although the going was very tough, Fuchs was very determined to complete his journey. He finally arrived at the Pole on the 19th of January.

His team spent a few days there and then took the route that Hillary and his team had marked out and supplied. They reached McMurdo Sound on the 2nd of March. They had done the entire trip across Antarctica in ninety-nine days.

Shackleton's dream, forty-four years earlier, was realised!

Hillary did something no one had done before. He invited everyone to help him find the money that was needed for his big adventure. Age didn't matter nor how little they could give. Two pounds or one thousand, loaves of bread or tractors – all counted and when everybody put in what they could give, there was enough for an exciting adventure.

In the Bible we find people of all ages doing things for Jesus. There were his disciples who travelled with him and helped him, men and women who gave money, a lady who washed his feet and dried it with her hair, women who cooked food for the meetings he spoke at, children who came to hear the stories he told, a little boy who gave Jesus his lunch so he could feed 5,000 people! Jesus loved them all and in one way or another they were all part of his 'team'. What can you do for Jesus today? Ask him. You may be surprised!

Keeping the Peace

As explorers slowly discovered some of Antarctica's treasures, many countries began to realise that Antarctica was a world resource and shouldn't belong to just one or two of them.

The 1950s were a time when the world was restless, people in many countries worried that war might break out again anytime and anywhere. Antarctica was in special danger. No one knew just what minerals and other treasures might be hidden under the ice and many countries wanted a part of it. They hoped it might give them special advantages in case of war.

So in the 1950s, American President Dwight D. Eisenhower invited all countries to sign an agreement to keep Antarctica as a place of peace and whatever anyone discovered there, should be shared openly. Everyone should have the freedom to do research there and share the results to help make the world a better place.

Twelve nations agreed to be part of an international agreement known as the Antarctic Treaty: Argentina, Australia, Belgium, Chile, Great Britain, Japan, New Zealand, Norway, South Africa, the Soviet Union and the United States all signed in 1959. Over the years many other countries joined them. Many of them built bases in Antarctica and ran research projects from them. They agreed to protect whales, seals, birds and other wildlife. Scientists work together to protect oil, natural gas and mineral resources. At the moment it is too expensive to drill for these in Antarctica, but that might change one day!

Today there are thirty-seven permanent bases run by seventeen nations and four more on subantarctic islands. In summer about 4,000 people live there; in winter, when it is totally dark, the population is about 1,000. These Antarctic 'settlers' include scientists, technicians and maintenance workers from all over the world. They all take great care of the environment and make sure their people don't leave garbage, sewage, or empty fuel containers at their bases.

They often make new discoveries. For example, in 1980, an American scientist, Bill Green, took a close look at five unusual lakes in the McMurdo Dry Valleys. These valleys are dry because the mountains above them stop ice from flowing into them and low snowfall and high winds leave the ground bare. The lakes are covered by a lid of ice (sometimes as thick as four meters), but not frozen solid all the way down under the ice. The water at the bottom is 25°C. This is opposite to other lakes in the world, where the top layers, being closer to the sun, are warmer than the bottom ones.

There are no fish in these lakes, but Green's team found algae, bacteria and yeasts. Over the years they made many more discoveries which help us to understand our world better. In fact, there was so much to learn that the International Council of

Scientific Unions declared the year starting in July 1957 as the International Geophysical Year (IGY).

Scientists from all over the world signed up for the IGY and agreed to take part in a series of coordinated observations of various geophysical phenomena. They studied everything they could think about – from astronomy to zoology. Their work was done in many countries across the globe, but especially in Antarctica.

Among the many things they discovered was that whales were in danger of becoming extinct and later, limits were placed on catching them. Studies of birds, seals and other wildlife are also making sure they don't disappear altogether.

No one knows whether oil, natural gas or minerals are hidden under the Antarctic Ice but in 1977 the Treaty partners agreed

not to drill for any of these. At the time there probably wasn't a lot of danger that any of them would, because oil and gas were available much cheaper in other parts of the world. But the time might come when those places run out and they could be looking at Antarctica. So they agreed they wouldn't do that.

More recently the problem of the world becoming warmer has become very important. Scientists noticed that some of Antarctica's ice shelves were breaking off and slowly melting. In 2002 a section of the Ross Ice Shelf – 47 miles (75.6 kilometres) long, 4.6 miles (7.4 kilometres) wide – broke off from the mainland. Water from melting glaciers flows into the oceans and they rise. There is concern that the water will flood some of the Pacific Islands and the people will have to move.

When God created man and woman he asked them and their descendants to take care of the earth (Gen. 1:28). He said to them:

> 'Be fruitful and increase in number; fill the earth and subdue it. Rule over the fish of the sea and the birds of the air and over every living creature that moves on the ground' (Gen. 1:28).

Then Adam and Eve disobeyed God and he threw them out of Eden. But he didn't tell them to stop looking after the earth.

It continued to be their responsibility and it is ours today. We are to love, care and be responsible for all of God's creation, but most of all we must love and care for each other.

Visitors to Antarctica

Today Antarctica is not just a place for explorers and scientists. Since the 1960s adventure-loving tourists have come during the summer to see the continent for themselves.

Most of them travel on cruise ships which are specially strengthened for the journey through the sea ice. These ships generally start from South America and sail across the sometimes treacherous Drake Passage to the Antarctic Peninsula. The trip takes two to three days.

As there are no tourist hotels or lodges in Antarctica they eat and sleep on the boat that brought them. Whenever possible they go ashore in small groups in inflatable boats known as Zodiacs. As there are no vehicles for tourists to drive or ride in, they have to walk once they land. They can visit some of the huts built by the early explorers, and get close enough to the wild life to take amazing pictures of four varieties of penguins (and walk among them), Weddell seals, sea lions, elephant seals, and numerous birds. But they are asked not to disturb the animals, nor dump garbage or sewage in the sea.

Traditionally, New Zealand harbours were the last port of call for Antarctic explorers and some of today's tourists like to do their trip from there too. It takes about three times as long as the tours from South America and rather than visit the Peninsula they go through the Ross Sea to McMurdo Sound.

New Zealanders, Neil and Barbara Robertson left from the most southern port of New Zealand (Bluff) on one of the smaller boats. It carried forty-nine passengers, twenty-two crew, eight guides and a cook. With such a small number of passengers everyone got lots of chances to go on land, the Robertsons

explained. They loved this because they had done a lot of study and there was a lot they wanted to see. Fortunately the weather was good so the Zodiacs could land them many times. Neil and Barbara were privileged to see Scott's hut.

In 1964 a four man team from New Zealand went to Antarctica to clean up this hut and the area around it. During their five weeks in Antarctica they stored all the records and papers they found there, sealed it against the cold winters and prepared the broken windows and noted other damage to be repaired the following season.

In 1977, both the Australian national airline and Air New Zealand started tourist sightseeing flights over Antarctica. They didn't land, but thrilled their passengers with the wonderful views.

Two years later, tragedy struck. One of the Air New Zealand flights crashed on Mount Erebus with the loss of all crew (20) and 237 passengers. It was the worst civil disaster in the history of New Zealand. It was also Air New Zealand's last tourist flight to Antarctica.

Qantas also stopped its flights but started again in 1994. They now offer flights about twelve times a year. There are also many flights from South America.

Why do people want to visit Antarctica? It is an adventure and like no other place in the world. It is remote, expensive and difficult to get to, so completely different from anywhere else in the world, an amazing wilderness with majestic mountains, glaciers, icebergs and fascinating wildlife.

Many Christians who experience this beauty believe that it helps them understand God better. One great Scottish naturalist said that while we must study God's Word, the Bible, we should look at nature as God's outdoor classroom and grow in our love for him by studying its beauty and majesty.

These words by the poet Henry G. Bosch might have been written about Antarctica:

O Lord, we can see all around us each day
The wisdom the creatures of nature display
O help us to learn from Your marvelous world
The wonder and beauty Your hands have unfurled.

To be in Antarctica makes people aware of the greatness of God in creation. Hopefully, it will be possible to keep it pure and beautiful.

Post Script

One hundred years after the first steps on the Pole.

In January 2012 special celebrations marked one hundred years since Robert Falcon Scott arrived at the South Pole in 1912.

As part of the celebrations in 2012, a team of workers travelled to Antarctica to repair Scott's hut which holds more than 10,000 artefacts from the 1910-1912 expedition.

Among the workers was Scott's grandson. Young Falcon Scott, who is a qualified builder, was proud to be part of the team.

'As a close relative, it's very important to me,' said Falcon. 'You can imagine a lot of things, but you can only get a real picture of it when you see it for yourself.'

Falcon provided a special link to the man with a dream who lost his life trying to achieve it.

Antarctic Map

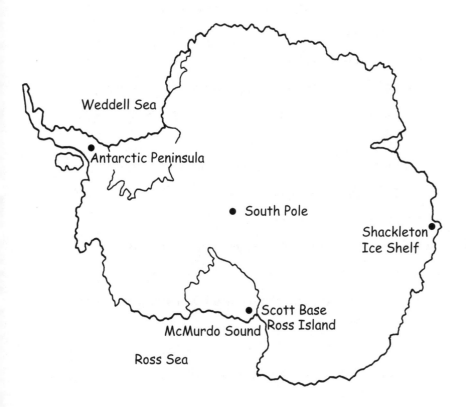

Weddell Sea

Antarctic Peninsula

South Pole

Shackleton
Ice Shelf

Scott Base
Ross Island

McMurdo Sound

Ross Sea

Antarctic Quiz

1. What was the name of the biscuit makers who made biscuits for British Antarctic Expeditions?

2. How much of the Antarctic continent is covered in ice?

3. Who was the Captain of the ship called *Endeavour*?

4. What was the name of the volcano discovered by John Ross?

5. Does God always answer our prayers immediately?

6. Name the team leaders in the race to the South Pole.

7. Which country won the race?

8. How should we respond when things go wrong in life?

9. How tall is an Emperor penguin?

10. What causes us to stray away from God?

11. In which year was the Magnetic North Pole discovered?

12. Who discovered the Magnetic South Pole?

13. In the Bible, what caused Paul and Barnabas to go their separate ways?

14. What are krill?

15. What does God promise those who love him will enjoy in the future?

16. What was the bronze statue which was placed on the grave of Henry McNeish?

17. In what ways does God want us to look after the environment?

18. What name was given to the mountain range Byrd and his men discovered in Antarctica?

19. What is the race that God tells us we should run?

20. For how many months is the sky over Antarctica dark?

21. What is the Antarctic equivalent of Aurora Borealis?

22. What did Ed Hillary and team arrive with in McMurdo Sound on 1st January 1957?

23. How many nations signed the Antarctic Treaty in 1959?

24. What is causing the ice shelves and glaciers to melt in the Antarctic?

25. What year was New Zealand's worst civil aviation disaster?

26. What helps us appreciate God more?

Antarctic Answers

1. Huntly and Palmer

2. 99%

3. Captain James Cook

4. Mount Erebus

5. No. Sometimes we have to wait.

6. Robert Scott (Britain) and Roald Amundsen (Norway).

7. Norway

8. Ask the question, 'What should I do now' and then move on.

9. 1.1 m

10. Worldly pleasures

11. 1831

12. Ernest Shackleton

13. A difference of opinion.

14. A kind of shrimp.

15. The right to eat from the tree of life.

16. Mrs Chippy

17. Take home rubbish, look after God's creatures, and don't be careless or wasteful.

18. Rockefeller Mountains

19. The plan he has set for us and the goals he wants us to achieve.

20. Four

21. The Aurora Australis

22. Eighteen men, sixty well-trained dogs, seven tractors and a Beaver reconnaissance plane.

23. Twelve

24. Global warming

25. 1979

26. Studying his creation

About the Author

Bartha Hill was a daughter of the manse: her father was a minister, her mother's parents were missionaries in Surinam and her father's father was also a parish minister.

Although she grew up in a Christian environment it was not till her early teens that she made a personal decision to invite Jesus to be her Lord and Saviour.

She trained to be a teacher and taught school for several years until she met Graham Hill, a young doctor with a missionary vision. They married and went to serve the Lord in Hong Kong and Indonesia until illness brought them home.

Over the next few years they worked in England and America, and finally settled back in their home country. Bartha started writing stories for a children's Christian magazine, became the south island correspondent for a Christian newspaper, and wrote the life stories of several missionaries. Her first book for children was published in 2007.

New Zealand has always been closely connected with Antarctica. It was often the final port for expeditions before heading south, and most of its citizens, including school children, have been fascinated by this exciting continent.

Bartha and Graham have three sons and eleven grandchildren. All are strongly involved in their churches.

Sample chapter
from Emerald Isle
Adventures
by Robert Plant

Emerald Isle

Ireland – the 'Emerald Isle' – situated off the west coast of Great Britain and covering an area of over 84,000 square kilometres, is one of the most picturesque countries in the world. It has 2,797 kilometres of coastline (not including all its islands) which varies from large sandy beaches and small sheltered bays, to high windswept cliffs, teaming with wildlife. Travelling through Ireland, you will notice that the predominant colour is green, giving rise to its being known around the world as the 'Emerald Isle'.

Did you know that Ireland is the twentieth largest island in the world and the second largest in Europe, after Britain (if you exclude Iceland)? Ireland consists of two countries and thirty two counties comprising twenty six in the south, known as the Republic of Ireland and six in the north, known as Northern Ireland or Ulster. Ireland was ruled as part of the United Kingdom until it was partitioned into the North and South in 1922, the south becoming a totally independent nation but the North remaining allied with Great Britain.

Having hundreds of kilometres of coastline, Ireland is greatly influenced by the sea, in terms of its wildlife, geography and geology. It is a land of mountains and lochs, rivers and rocks, leprechauns and giants! Ireland also contains one of the most interesting and captivating histories of any land on earth, reaching right back to Norman times.

Have you heard of the term 'The Troubles'? This was a thirty year period of unrest, at the close of the last century, mainly between the Catholic and Protestant communities. They were divided about whether Ireland should remain as two countries or be united as one, under the flag of the southern Republic. Sadly, during this period of upheaval, many hundreds of people died in shootings and bombings, as both sides were guilty of committing the most horrendous atrocities. Thankfully, since what was called the 'Good Friday Agreement' was signed in 1998 and the introduction of the even newer power-sharing executive ruling Northern Ireland from Stormont (its capital building), those sad and deadly days are past.

Today there are only a few extremists, still wanting to resort to violent methods, in order to get their way. The legacy of these times, however, continues to live on, in many people's minds as they remember terrible news headlines from these dark days. Sadly, most of these people have never visited Ireland and can only associate it with 'The Troubles'. I hope, as you read this book, you will discover what a beautiful and exciting place the Emerald Isle really is.

It is a country which has produced some of the most famous writers, scientists and intellectuals in the world, as well as laying claim to having had twenty three American Presidents, with

Irish ancestry. The grandfather of famous American actress Grace Kelly, who later became Princess of Monaco, was born in Ireland. Once married and known as Princess Grace of Monaco, she made a hobby of collecting Irish books and music. By the time of her untimely death in a car accident in 1981, her library contained over eight thousand titles. This extensive collection can still be seen in her hometown of Monaco, at the Princess Grace Irish Library.

We have included a 'Things to Do and See' section for the majority of the chapters, however it is worth checking the opening times of these places, as they do vary widely.

So, come with me on a journey up high mountains, along winding rivers, through picturesque towns, offshore to isolated islands, and descending deep underground as well as getting up close and personal with some famous sons and daughters of Ireland.

The Adventures Series
An ideal series to collect

Have you ever wanted to visit the rainforest? Have you ever longed to sail down the Amazon river? Would you just love to go on Safari in Africa? Well these books can help you imagine that you are actually there.

Pioneer missionaries retell their amazing adventures and encounters with animals and nature. In the Amazon you will discover tree frogs, piranha fish and electric eels. In the Rainforest you will be amazed at the armadillo and the toucan. In the blistering heat of the African Savannah you will come across lions, elephants and hyenas. And you will discover how God is at work in these amazing environments.

African Adventures by Dick Anderson
ISBN 978-1-85792-807-5
Amazon Adventures by Horace Banner
ISBN 978-1-85792-440-4
Antarctic Adventures by Bartha Hill
ISBN 978-1-78191-135-8
Cambodian Adventures by Donna Vann
ISBN 978-1-84550-474-8
Emerald Isle Adventures by Robert Plant
ISBN 978-1-78191-136-5
Great Barrier Reef Adventures by Jim Cromarty
ISBN 978-1-84550-068-9
Himalayan Adventures by Penny Reeve
ISBN 978-1-84550-080-1
Kiwi Adventures by Bartha Hill
ISBN 978-1-84550-282-9
New York City Adventures by Donna Vann
ISBN 978-1-84550-546-2
Outback Adventures by Jim Cromarty
ISBN 978-1-85792-974-4
Pacific Adventures by Jim Cromarty
ISBN 978-1-84550-475-5
Rainforest Adventures by Horace Banner
ISBN 978-1-85792-627-9
Rocky Mountain Adventures by Betty Swinford
ISBN 978-1-85792-962-1
Scottish Highland Adventures by Catherine Mackenzie
ISBN 978-1-84550-281-2
Wild West Adventures by Donna Vann
ISBN 978-1-84550-065-8

Jungle Doctor on Safari by Paul White
ISBN 978-1-84550-391-8

Yet again the Jungle Doctor is in the thick of a battle for people's lives. There is so much that good medicine can do to tackle injuries and disease, yet local customs and superstition hold back the hospital staff at one mission hospital from saving one woman's life. The doctors and nurses have to work in poor operating conditions, with very limited equipment and drugs, but despite everything, other lives are saved! However, sometimes it seems that everything is going wrong; especially when the old hospital car continues to break down. But throughout it all, the Jungle Doctor and his staff know that God answers prayer! A thrilling adventure from Paul White based in Mvumi hospital, Tanzania.

THE JUNGLE DOCTOR SERIES

1. Jungle Doctor and the Whirlwind
    978-1-84550-296-6
2. Jungle Doctor on the Hop
    978-1-84550-297-3
3. Jungle Doctor Spots a Leopard
    978-1-84550-301-7
4. Jungle Doctor's Crooked Dealings
    978-1-84550-299-7
5. Jungle Doctor's Enemies
    978-1-84550-300-0
6. Jungle Doctor in Slippery Places
    978-1-84550-298-0
7. Jungle Doctor's Africa
    978-1-84550-388-8
8. Jungle Doctor on Safari
    978-1-84550-391-8
9. Jungle Doctor Meets a Lion
    978-1-84550-392-5
10. Eyes on Jungle Doctor
    978-1-84550-393-2
11. Jungle Doctor Stings a Scorpion
    978-1-84550-390-1
12. Jungle Doctor Pulls a Leg
    978-1-84550-389-5
13. Jungle Doctor Looks for Trouble
    978-1-84550-499-1
14. Jungle Doctor Operates
    978-1-84550-500-4
15. Jungle Doctor to the Rescue
    978-1-84550-516-5
16. Jungle Doctor Attacks Witchcraft
    978-1-84550-517-2
17. Jungle Doctor Goes West
    978-1-84550-595-0
18. Jungle Doctor Sees Red
    978-1-84550-501-1
19. Jungle Doctor's Case Book
    978-1-84550-502-8

CHRISTIAN FOCUS PUBLICATIONS

Christian Christian CF4K Mentor
Focus Heritage

Christian Focus Publications publishes books for adults and children under its four main imprints: Christian Focus, Christian Heritage, CF4K and Mentor. Our books reflect that God's word is reliable and Jesus is the way to know him, and live for ever with him.

Our children's publication list includes a Sunday school curriculum that covers pre-school to early teens; puzzle and activity books. We also publish personal and family devotional titles, biographies and inspirational stories that children will love.

If you are looking for quality Bible teaching for children then we have an excellent range of Bible story and age specific theological books. From pre-school to teenage fiction, we have it covered!

Find us at our web page:
www.christianfocus.com

CF4 •K
Because you're never
too young to know Jesus